Knowbuddy

.50

Venus

Revised Edition

by Steven L. Kipp

Consultant:
Gregory L. Vogt
Teaching from Space Program
Oklahoma State University

Bridgestone Books
an imprint of Capstone Press
Mankato, Minnesota

Bridgestone Books are published by Capstone Press
151 Good Counsel Drive, P.O. Box 669, Mankato, Minnesota 56002
http://www.capstone-press.com

Library of Congress Cataloging-in-Publication Data
The Library of Congress has cataloged the first edition as follows:
Kipp, Steven L.
    Venus/by Steven L. Kipp.
    p. cm.—(The galaxy)
    Includes bibliographical references and index.
    Summary: Discusses the orbit, atmosphere, surface features, exploration, and other
aspects of the planet Venus.
    ISBN 0-7368-0519-2
    1. Venus (Planet)—Juvenile literature. [1. Venus (Planet)] I. Title. II. Series.
QB621.K57 1998
523.42—dc21
                                                                    97-6923
                                                                    CIP

Editorial Credits
Tom Adamson, editor; Timothy Halldin, cover designer and illustrator; Kimberly Danger
    and Jodi Theisen, photo researchers

Photo Credits
NASA, cover, 1, 10, 12, 16, 20
NASA/JPL, 14, 18
NASA/USGS, 8
Steven L. Kipp, 6

1 2 3 4 5 6 05 04 03 02 01 00

Table of Contents

Relative size of the Sun and the planets

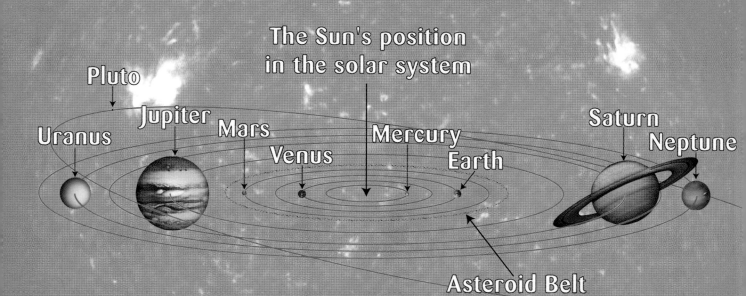

Pluto

Uranus

Jupiter

Mars

Venus

The Sun's position in the solar system

Mercury

Earth

Saturn

Neptune

Asteroid Belt

The Sun

Venus is a planet in the solar system. The Sun is the center of the solar system. Planets, asteroids, and comets travel around the Sun.

Venus is one of four inner planets that have rocky surfaces. Mercury, Earth, and Mars are the other inner planets. The outer planets are Jupiter, Saturn, Uranus, and Neptune. These giant planets are made of gases. Pluto is the farthest planet from the Sun. It is made of rock and ice.

Venus is the hottest planet in the solar system. The surface temperature on Venus can reach 900 degrees Fahrenheit (480 degrees Celsius).

◀ **This illustration compares the sizes of the planets and the Sun. Venus is slightly smaller than Earth. The blue lines show the orbits of the planets. Thousands of asteroids move around the Sun. The asteroid belt is between the orbits of Mars and Jupiter.**

At certain times of the year, people can see Venus at sunrise.

Venus is the second planet from the Sun. It is about 67 million miles (108 million kilometers) away from the Sun.

From Earth, Venus is the third brightest object in the sky. Only the Sun and Earth's Moon are brighter. From Earth, Venus looks like a bright star. In space, Venus is a white-yellow color.

Venus is called the evening star when it appears in the western sky after sunset. Venus sometimes is visible in the eastern sky before sunrise. At these times, Venus is known as the morning star.

All planets except Earth are named for characters in Greek or Roman myths. In these ancient stories, Venus was the Roman goddess of love. This symbol stands for the planet Venus.

FAST FACTS

	Venus	Earth
Diameter:	7,521 miles (12,104 kilometers)	7,927 miles (12,756 kilometers)
Average distance from the Sun:	67 million miles (108 million kilometers)	93 million miles (150 million kilometers)
Revolution period:	225 days	365 days, 6 hours
Rotation period:	243 days, spins backwards	23 hours, 56 minutes
Moons:	0	1

People sometimes call Venus Earth's twin. Earth and Venus are about the same size. Earth is 7,927 miles (12,756 kilometers) wide. Venus is 7,521 miles (12,104 kilometers) wide. Venus also is the closest planet to Earth. But the two planets are more different than they are alike.

Most planets have a mixture of gases surrounding them called an atmosphere. Scientists once thought Venus might have an atmosphere like Earth's. But Venus's atmosphere is much thicker and is made up of different gases.

Scientists once thought Venus might have oceans like Earth. But Venus has no water at all. Living things need water to survive. Life as we know it could not exist on Venus.

The colors in this picture show elevation on Venus. Blue areas are low plains. Brown areas are mountainous regions.

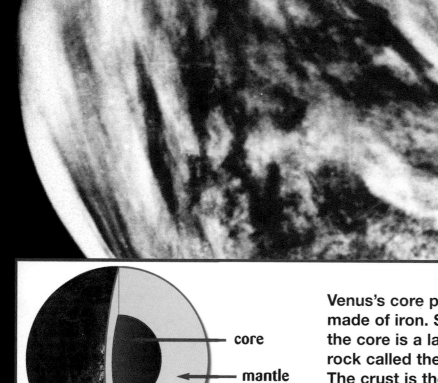

core

mantle

crust

Venus's core probably is made of iron. Surrounding the core is a layer of liquid rock called the mantle. The crust is the outer layer. The crust is made of lightweight rocks.

Gases make up Venus's atmosphere. Carbon dioxide is the main gas in the planet's atmosphere. People breathe out carbon dioxide and breathe in oxygen. Venus's atmosphere has very little oxygen. People could not breathe on Venus.

Thick clouds made of sulfuric acid form part of Venus's atmosphere. On Venus, rain falls as sulfuric acid instead of water. But the sulfuric acid does not reach the ground because the planet is so hot. Heat turns the sulfuric acid back into a gas. The gas rises into the clouds again.

Venus's atmosphere is very heavy. The weight of the atmosphere puts pressure on the planet. This pressure can crush objects that enter the planet's atmosphere.

The atmosphere of Venus has very thick clouds.

The illustration at the left shows how the greenhouse effect works on Venus. The yellow arrows show sunlight. The red arrows are heat trapped in Venus's atmosphere. Only a little heat escapes Venus's thick atmosphere.

A greenhouse is a building made of glass. People grow plants in greenhouses. The glass lets in light from the Sun. The light heats up the soil and plants. The glass does not let much of the heat escape. The air inside stays warm. This process is called the greenhouse effect.

The greenhouse effect happens on Venus. Venus's thick carbon dioxide atmosphere holds in most of the Sun's heat. The atmosphere lets only a little heat escape.

Venus is the hottest of all the planets. Scientists discovered that the average temperature on Venus is about 900 degrees Fahrenheit (480 degrees Celsius). This temperature is 400 degrees Fahrenheit (200 degrees Celsius) hotter than most ovens can reach. Liquid water cannot exist on a planet with such hot temperatures.

The greenhouse effect makes Venus's surface very hot.

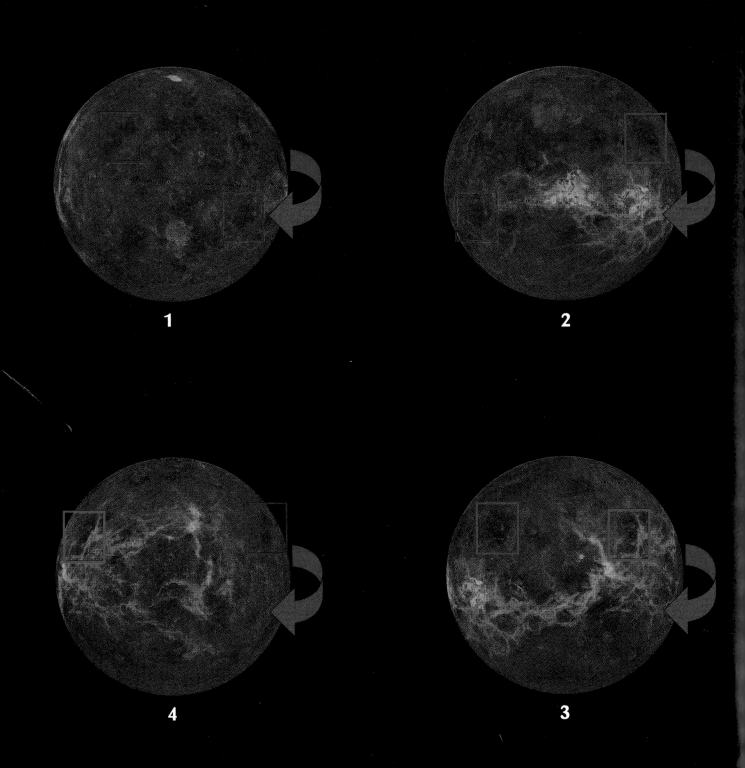

Like all planets, Venus travels around the Sun in a path called an orbit. One complete orbit is called a revolution. Venus makes one revolution around the Sun every 225 days.

Venus also spins as it orbits. One complete spin is called a rotation. Venus rotates very slowly. The planet makes one rotation every 243 days. This rotation time is slower than any other planet.

Venus rotates in the opposite direction of most other planets. Venus rotates from east to west. The Sun rises in the west and sets in the east on Venus. The opposite is true on Earth and most of the other planets.

Venus's revolution and rotation speed help scientists measure its solar day. The solar day is the time from one sunrise to the next sunrise. Venus's solar day is equal to 117 days on Earth.

These four views of Venus show the planet as it rotates. Astronomers observe the planet's rotation by comparing the positions of different surface features.

Galileo Galilei was a famous astronomer who lived during the 1600s. He was the first astronomer to look at Venus through a telescope.

Galileo discovered that Venus seemed to change shape. But Venus does not really change shape. The Sun lights only part of the planet at a time. From Earth, people can see only the part of Venus that the Sun lights. This part is called a phase.

Venus sometimes passes between the Sun and Earth. This movement is called a transit. People can see transits only with special telescopes. The telescopes filter out the Sun's bright light. During a transit, Venus looks like a small spot moving across the Sun.

Transits of Venus are very uncommon. They occur in pairs about eight years apart. The next transits will be on June 8, 2004, and June 6, 2012. Another pair of transits will not happen until December 11, 2117, and December 8, 2125.

These pictures show different phases of Venus. People can see the phases of Venus through a telescope.

Venera space probes were the first spacecraft to land on Venus. The Soviet Union sent these space probes to Venus in the 1970s. The pressure of Venus's thick atmosphere quickly crushed the space probes.

The space probes sent a few TV pictures of Venus to Earth. The pictures showed that flat rocks with sharp edges cover Venus. These rocks are similar to volcanic rocks on Earth.

Venus also has craters. The craters formed when meteorites crashed into Venus. Meteorites are pieces of large space rocks that hit a planet's or a moon's surface.

The sunlight that travels through Venus's clouds makes the sky look orange. From Venus's surface, the sky is always the color of a sunrise or a sunset on Earth.

Lava flows and craters cover most of the surface of Venus.

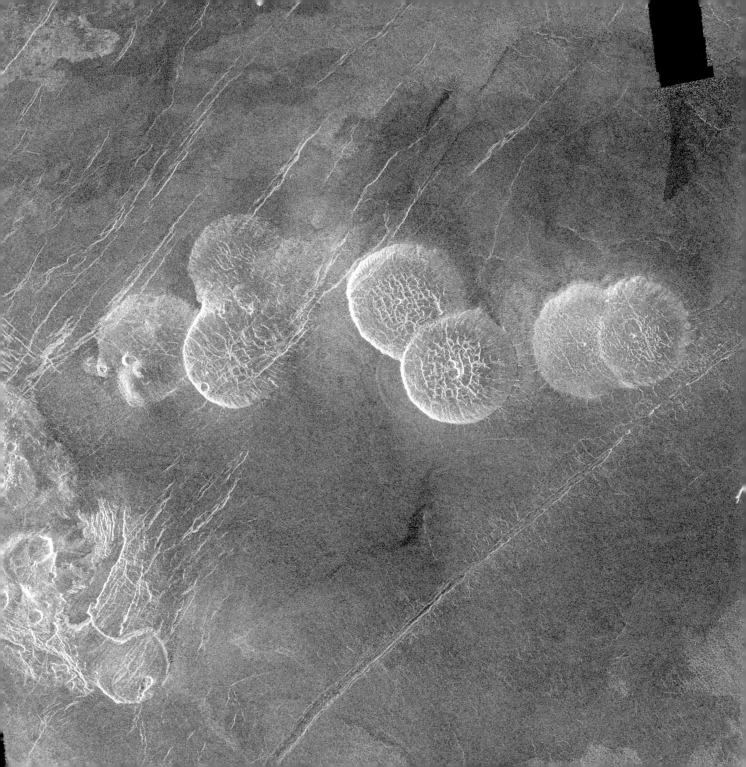

Magellan

The *Magellan* space probe orbited Venus from 1990 to 1994. This U.S. spacecraft used radar to map the surface of Venus. Radar uses radio waves. The radio waves bounce off the planet and give readings of the land.

Magellan sent back pictures of Venus's surface. They showed many large craters and volcanoes. Volcanoes are vents, or openings, in a planet's surface. When a volcano erupts, gases and liquid rock called lava explode through the opening. Most of Venus is covered with hardened lava.

Some areas of Venus are flat. Higher places rise above the flat land. Scientists call these areas continents. A few mountains rise from the continents.

Scientists still have questions about Venus. They hope to learn more about Venus in future space missions.

Some volcanoes on Venus appear flat. Astronomers call them pancake volcanoes.

Hands On: The Greenhouse Effect

The greenhouse effect makes Venus a hot planet. You can make a small greenhouse and grow plants in it. This experiment will show how the greenhouse effect works.

What You Need

A glass or plastic jar with a lid
Potting soil
About ten plant seeds
Water

What You Do

1. Take the lid off the jar.
2. Put 2 inches (5 centimeters) of soil in the bottom of the jar.
3. Sprinkle the seeds on the soil.
4. Cover the seeds with 1 inch (2.5 centimeters) of soil.
5. Sprinkle a little water on the soil.
6. Place the lid back on the jar.
7. Place your jar in a sunny place.

The jar works like Venus's atmosphere. It will trap the Sun's heat. The inside of your greenhouse will become warm. This heat will help the plants grow.

Words to Know

atmosphere (AT-muhss-feehr)—the mixture of gases that surrounds some planets

crater (KRAY-tur)—a hole in the ground made by a meteorite

greenhouse effect (GREEN-houss uh-FEKT)—the trapping of heat by a thick atmosphere or glass

meteorite (MEE-tee-ur-rite)—a piece of space rock that strikes a planet or a moon

phases (FAZE-ess)—the different parts of a moon or planet lit up by the Sun

revolution (rev-uh-LOO-shuhn)—the movement of one object around another object in space

rotation (roh-TAY-shuhn)—one complete spin of an object in space

space probe (SPAYSS PROHB)—a spacecraft that travels to other planets and outer space

telescope (TEL-uh-skope)—an instrument that makes faraway objects seem larger and closer

Read More

Brimner, Larry Dane. *Venus.* A True Book. New York: Children's Press, 1998.

Kerrod, Robin. *Astronomy.* Young Scientist Concepts and Projects. Milwaukee: Gareth Stevens, 1998.

Simon, Seymour. *Venus.* New York: Mulberry Books, 1998.

Useful Addresses

Canadian Space Agency
6767 Route de l'Aéroport
Saint-Hubert, QC J3Y 8Y9
Canada

NASA Headquarters
Washington, DC 20546-0001

The Planetary Society
65 Catalina Avenue
Pasadena, CA 91106-2301

Internet Sites

The Nine Planets
http://www.tcsn.net/afiner
The Space Place
http://spaceplace.jpl.nasa.gov/spacepl.htm
StarChild
http://starchild.gsfc.nasa.gov/docs/StarChild/
    StarChild.html

Index